MW01165100

JUL        ....

# GENIES

**DiscoverRoo**
An Imprint of Pop!
popbooksonline.com

Martha London

abdobooks.com

Published by Pop!, a division of ABDO, PO Box 398166,
Minneapolis, Minnesota 55439. Copyright © 2020 by POP,
LLC. International copyrights reserved in all countries. No
part of this book may be reproduced in any form without
written permission from the publisher. Pop!™ is a trademark
and logo of POP, LLC.

Printed in the United States of America, North Mankato,
Minnesota.

102019
012020

THIS BOOK CONTAINS
RECYCLED MATERIALS

Cover Photo: iStockphoto
Interior Photos: iStockphoto, 1, 5, 6–7 (genie), 7 (scroll), 9,
11, 12, 15, 16 (bottom), 21, 28; Shutterstock Images, 8, 16
(top), 19, 20 (top), 20 (bottom), 23, 26–27, 30; Edmund Dulac/
AF Fotografie/Alamy, 13, 24–25; Pictorial Press Ltd./Alamy,
17 (top); Walt Disney/AF archive/Alamy, 17 (bottom); Walt
Disney/Lifestyle pictures/Alamy, 29

Editor: Sophie Geister-Jones
Series Designer: Jake Nordby

Library of Congress Control Number: 2019942461

Publisher's Cataloging-in-Publication Data

Names: London, Martha, author.

Title: Genies / by Martha London

Description: Minneapolis, Minnesota : Pop!, 2020 | Series:
Mythical creatures | Includes online resources and index.

Identifiers: ISBN 9781532165764 (lib. bdg.) | ISBN
9781532167089 (ebook)

Subjects: LCSH: Mythical animals--Juvenile literature. |
Genies--Juvenile literature. | Folklore--Juvenile
literature. | Legends--Juvenile literature. | Animals and
history--Juvenile literature.

Classification: DDC 398.45--dc23

Marzo
J

# WELCOME TO DiscoverRoo!

Pop open this book and you'll find QR codes loaded

with information, so you can learn even more!

Scan this code* and others

like it while you read, or visit

the website below to make

this book pop!

## popbooksonline.com/genies

*Scanning QR codes requires a web-enabled smart device with a QR code reader app and a camera.

# TABLE OF CONTENTS

# CHAPTER 1
# AN UNEXPECTED CATCH

Early one morning, a girl went fishing by a river. She cast her line out over the water. Then she waited. Suddenly, she felt a tug. When she pulled the line in, her hook held a small pot.

WATCH A VIDEO HERE!

Today, many people imagine that pots for coffee or tea are homes for genies.

She opened its lid.
Smoke streamed out and
formed the shape of a
person. It was a
genie!

"Thank you for finding me," he said.

"I will give you two wishes."

The girl was excited. But she knew

she had to be careful. Genies could be

tricky.

The girl thought. Then she said,

"First, I wish this pot will fill with food

whenever I ask. Second, I wish you can

go free."

The girl kept the pot, the genie went

free, and both of them were happy.

In ancient stories, travelers often found genies by accident.

## CHAPTER 2
# MADE FROM FIRE

Tales of genies have existed for

thousands of years. But **ancient** stories

did not always say genies granted wishes.

Instead, the **legends** changed over time.

The first stories came from the

LEARN MORE
HERE!

*Stories of genies began in ancient Mesopotamia.*

**Middle East**, northern Africa, and southeastern Asia.

In Islam, genies are called jinn. Islamic texts say God created the jinn with fire. People throughout the Middle East wrote and told stories about these beings. Some were

*Jinn were made from fire that did not create any smoke.*

part of a famous book called *One Thousand and One Nights*. This book's **narrator** tells many stories to a king.

**ONE THOUSAND AND ONE NIGHTS**

*One Thousand and One Nights* is a collection of many stories. The stories were created and collected over hundreds of years. Some of the most famous stories tell about Aladdin, Ali Baba, and Sinbad the Sailor. But these stories weren't in early versions of the book. European translators added them later.

*A character named Scheherazade is the narrator of* One Thousand and One Nights.

As Islam spread to new parts of the world, stories from *One Thousand and One Nights* spread too. The stories were **translated** to languages such as French and English. The translators changed some of the stories. And they added others. In the new stories, genies granted wishes to people.

# SPREAD OF ISLAM AND STORIES OF GENIES

Islam began in the Middle East in 622 CE. It later spread to Northern Africa and parts of Europe.

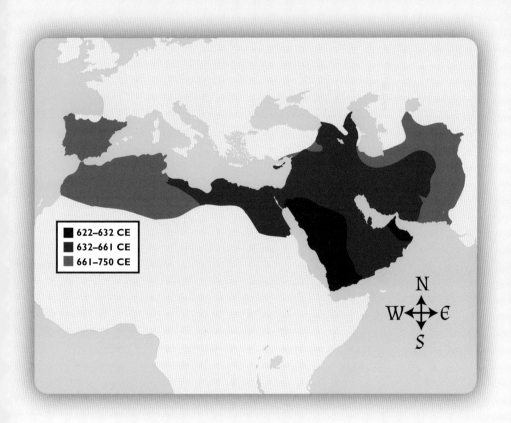

622–632 CE
632–661 CE
661–750 CE

# GENIES THROUGH THE YEARS

## 1000 CE
The book *One Thousand and One Nights* is written. It tells stories about jinn.

## 1704
*One Thousand and One Nights* is translated into French.

## 1800s
Stories about genies spread. The stories are about genies who grant wishes and are trapped in lamps.

**1965**

The TV show *I Dream of Jeannie* begins. It is about the life of a female genie.

**1900**

A French company makes a silent movie about the story of Aladdin.

**1992**

Disney creates an animated movie called *Aladdin*. It features a blue genie trapped in a lamp.

# CHAPTER 3
# MANY SHAPES

**Legends** say genies are usually

**invisible**. But genies are shape-shifters.

They can change their size or shape.

They can switch into humans or animals.

## DID YOU KNOW?

In many stories, genies change into snakes.

While most stories show genies as men, some stories feature female genies.

COMPLETE AN ACTIVITY HERE!

However, genies do not stay in these forms for long. Genies cannot be hurt when they are invisible. But if the form they take can be injured, so can the genie.

*Some genies chose to take the form of dogs or birds.*

*Sandstorms can make it so hard to see that people get lost.*

Some genies take the form of winds.

These genies are found in deserts. They

can cause sandstorms.

# CHAPTER 4
# MAGIC IN THE WORLD

Most genies try to avoid humans. They often live in ruins of buildings or other places far away from people. Genies also hide or turn **invisible**. They can shrink to fit in small spaces like lamps. They can even hide in trees and rocks.

LEARN MORE HERE!

Some stories say genies can be funny and helpful. Other stories say they are mean and wild.

When genies do meet people, they often play tricks on them. Sometimes they even make people sick.

In some cultures, genies are believed to cause illness. In 2015, people blamed genies when nine middle-school students **fainted** in a Saudi Arabian school.

*Some stories describe ways that people can summon a genie.*

A few genies choose to help people.

But it is not easy to get a genie to grant

a wish. Some **legends** say only a wizard

can control a genie.

*Some genies are tricked into lamps. Then, they have to do whatever the owner of the lamp says.*

Others say people have to wear a

magic ring. People may also get wishes by

finding a lamp where a genie is hiding.

*Sometimes genies take the form of a column of smoke.*

Over the years, stories about genies have changed. But genies continue to capture people's imagination.

*In the 2019 movie* Aladdin, *the genie takes the shape of a blue human.*

**DID YOU KNOW?**

Since 1900, more than 50 movies have been made that include a genie.

# MAKING CONNECTIONS

### TEXT-TO-SELF

In some stories, genies have the power to grant wishes. What is one thing you would wish for?

### TEXT-TO-TEXT

Have you read another book that mentioned genies? What were the genies in that book like?

### TEXT-TO-WORLD

Stories of genies began in the Middle East. What do you know about this part of the world?

# GLOSSARY

**ancient** – from a long time ago.

**faint** – to fall down because the brain does not get enough oxygen.

**invisible** – unable to be seen.

**legend** – a story passed down over many years.

**Middle East** – the part of the world where Africa and Asia meet.

**narrator** – the person who tells a story.

**translate** – to take a word or a sentence in one language and say it in another so a person can understand.

# INDEX

# ONLINE RESOURCES
## popbooksonline.com

Scan this code* and others like it while you read, or visit the website below to make this book pop!

## popbooksonline.com/genies

*Scanning QR codes requires a web-enabled smart device with a QR code reader app and a camera.